knowing You

SHAZIYA BARKAT

Copyright © 2019 Shaziya Barkat

All rights reserved. No part of this book may be reproduced in any form without written permission from the author.

ISBN: 978-1-0756-0251-1

READER TESTIMONIALS

"I wish there was a way for me to embrace you and tell you how much good your words brought to me. Thank you."
- *Ayesha* (Muslim Youth Musings)

"I feel that the author understood my exact struggles and helped me find a connection with my Creator that I was yearning for." - *Shereen Salama*

"...such beautiful writing with words from the heart!"
- *Fatima Az-Zahraa* (Muslim Youth Musings)

DEDICATION

To my *Lord*, all good comes only from You.

To my *parents,* for your continuous support, encouragement, and love.

CONTENTS

1 Introduction 1

2 Knowing You 3

3 Discovering Hope 21

4 Finding Me 43

5 Personal Narratives & Essays 75

INTRODUCTION

knowing You is about heartbreaks, loss, hope, and love. It is a spiritual reflection to return to a better, truer version of yourself through knowing God in all His glory. It is about overcoming your struggles, your disappointments, and your mistakes by finding your worth through faith. This book provides an uplifting spiritual renewal to build yourself back up in times when you feel damaged, broken, and hopeless by reflecting on God's attributes.

According to Islamic tradition, there are at least 99 names of *Allah* (the Arabic term for *God*), which describe His greatest attributes.

"The most beautiful names belong to Allah (God) so call on Him by them." (Quran 7:180)

This collection of poetry, prose, personal narratives, and essays is tailored to each of those names. Because it is in knowing Him, that we find who we truly are.

Abu Hurairah (may Allah be pleased with him) reported that Muhammad, peace and blessings be upon him, said:

"Allah has 99 names and whoever preserves them will enter paradise."
(Sahih Muslim 2677)

Hadith scholar Imam Nawawi comments on this, saying:

"To preserve them is said to mean to enumerate and count them in one's supplication by them. It is said it means to persevere in them, to respect them in the best manner, to guard what they require, and to affirm their meanings. And it is said the meaning is to act by them and to obey Allah according to the implications of every name."

Each of the names of Allah may have many manifestations. The work presented is a self-reflection of the author's understanding of these names. And Allah knows best.

knowing You

KNOWING YOU

if my words were stars
and i wrote Your praises
across the night sky
the sky would plummet down
by the weight of those words,
for even the universe is not enough
to encompass all of Your praises

Al-Hamid, Al-Aliyy: The Praiseworthy, The Exalted

KNOWING YOU

oh heavens,
how strong must our Lord be
to hold you up above
layer upon layer
like the petals of a rose
waiting to bloom
and welcome their visitors
with the sweetest of fragrances

Al-Qawi, Al- Aziz: The Possessor of All Strength, The Mighty

i see praises of You
alongside the seashore
and amidst the salty breeze
that sways the palm trees
to bow down in submission

i hear praises of You
among the moonlit sky
when i whisper prayers to the ground,
only to hear the nightingales
echo them towards the heavens

i feel praises of You
dwelling in my heart,
as it sways
from fear
to hope,
settling on peace and incomparable love

As-Salam: The Perfect Source of Peace

KNOWING YOU

there is a stillness in the hour
as sunlight pours through windows
like thick honey
into my cup of tea
milk descends smoothly from the skies
as intricately fashioned snowflakes
dissolving as they touch the brim
oh how Glorious is my Lord
for allowing me to witness the purity
of heaven's drinks
on this earth

Al-Maajid, Al-Majid: The Glorious, The Most Glorious

maybe,
that's what life is.
a mere collection of hellos
and goodbyes
as we grip onto photographs,
lockets kept near our hearts
holding onto each moment
each face
each feeling
as if the frame can imprison time,
immortalizing all that we fear to lose
as if our hands can forever grasp
onto all that is rushing back
to the Everlasting One

Al-Awwal, Al-Aakhir, Al-Baqi, Al-Hayy, As-Samad:
The First, The Last, The Everlasting, The Ever Living, the Eternal

KNOWING YOU

i placed my hand over my heart
and asked

> *to whom do you belong?*

it beat

> *Him*
>
> *Him*
>
> *Him*

Al-Malik, Al-Muta'ali: The Ultimate King, The Most High

if i were to tell the rivers
of the majesty of my Lord
the rivers would become shy
because in comparison to them,
my Lord's majesty runs much further

if i were to tell the mountains
of the glory of my Lord
the mountains would become consumed by humility
because in front of my Lord's glory,
even the mountains lose their stature

Al-Jalil, Al-Azeem: The Majestic, The Supreme Glory

KNOWING YOU

the canvas of our heart
we fill with so much -
people, possessions, and pride
only to have it be spoiled
by a color, a love, misplaced

our painting, now tainted.

we forget
that this canvas
and all that is on it
belongs to the Artist
and all that we love
manifests with Him

we are mesmerized by the elements
composing the masterpiece
yet without the Master,
it is left
just an empty,
blank canvas

Malik-al-Mulk: The Master of All Kingdoms

a sun resides in your chest,
rising and falling
by the command of your Lord
expanding and contracting your lungs
like the wings of birds in flight
each breath in its due measure
given,
each breath in its due measure,
taken.

Al-Basit, Al Qabid: The Expander, The Constrictor

KNOWING YOU

young, bright laughter
warmth from the windowpane
rays shining through and through
blue skies and painted planes
life peeking in through curtains
calling you to play
a youth that wants to last forever
a summer that's reluctant to stay

a period of growth
leaves changing colors before your eyes
from orange to yellow to red
leave yourself behind in nature's dyes
mistakes and moving on
identity still being found
a season that's dynamic
a fall so profound

weakened from age
bare trees frosted with winter snow
awaiting the final time
their skeletal hands protrude through a white glow
the forest so thick
as one slowly decays away
leaving behind nothing but memories
of the shade they had provided yesterday

as the land is left drenched
and the ice begins to melt
a start of a new life
a spring in hearts again felt

Al-Muhyi: The Giver of Life

and if our eyes cannot stand the direct sight of the sun -
a burning lamp that He has cast upon this earth,
how marvelous must the sight of the One
who has compelled it to shine be?

Al-Qahhar, Al-Jabbar: The All-Compelling Subduer, The Compeller

KNOWING YOU

i believe in my Lord
like i believe in the morning sun -
on some days it may be so strong
that its rays reflect off the waters
and cause the sand to scorch my feet
while on other days
it may be hidden beneath the clouds
its light veiled from others

but there is no doubt
that in either case
it is ever present
ever shining.

it is only my own vision that sometimes dims
it is only my own faith that sometimes needs strength

Az-Zaahir, Al-Baatin: The Manifest, The Hidden

i am the crescent moon.
a part of me, visible for those on earth to see
but understood, in whole,
only by the One who perceives all

Al-Waaijd, Al-Basir: The All-Perceiving, The All-Seer

KNOWING YOU

and the time will come
when you've exhausted your soul
and it'll yearn to return
home

Al-Warith: The Inheritor

and who else,
but the One
can compel the beaming sun to shine during the day
and then fashion it into tiny fireflies
to illuminate even the darkest corners of this earth
during the night

Al-Ahad, Al-Waahid: The Unique, The Only One

KNOWING YOU

Discovering Hope

KNOWING YOU

thick ash closed around him
clouding up his gaze
as he looked in a mirror,
an attempt to make out his face
scars marked near his heart
forever embedding his mistakes
tried to make it home
but lost in a haze

he was lost in an unreality
far away from his own
searching and fumbling through dark alleys
he scrounged all alone
until a call echoed out that he's perfectly imperfect
that the scars on his chest would soon be worth it
if he acknowledged what happened and what was to be
to realize, to admit, was needed to break free

he looked at the sky
at each wrongful action piled up into the night
a tear escaped down his cheek
as he thought he'd lost the ultimate fight
as that single drop met the floor and made a light patter
the pile that had risen to the skies
came

    down with

        a clatter.

Ar-Rahman, Ar-Raheem: The Most Gracious, The Most Merciful

and if He can take the dry, barren lands
that carpet the earth
and revive them again with rain
what makes you think
He can't do the same
with your heart?

Al-Ba'ith: The Resurrector

meet Him in the land
of your dreams and fears
show Him the skies
that disperse your troubled tears
when the winds whisper thoughts
that occupy your mind
show Him the world
in which you are confined
dig up the dirt
so you may see your roots
and how far you've come
to sow and reap your fruits
and if you find this world
weakening your faith, your foundation
seek Him over and over
through deeper conversations

Al-Wali, Al-Waali: The Protecting Friend, The Friendly Lord

my dear,
why do you place your heart
into the hands of those
not worthy of holding it

they are but waves
their reach extends only so much
rolling in
like a soft kiss to the sand
then leaving in just a moment's time

my dear,
why do you search for a love
that breaks you over and over again

bottle up your love
secure it with a cork
and with trust in your Lord
let it float away, preserved.

for when the time comes
He'll float it back to you
with a love that reflects His

a love that pours
from His endless vessel

a love much purer
than the salt water
that you drown yourself in

Al-Wadud: The Loving One

feel the blood flowing
as rivers through your veins
because heaven also has gardens
beneath which rivers flow
and *you* are the most beautiful garden
i have ever seen

Al-Musawwir: The Shaper of Beauty

KNOWING YOU

the dawn breaks every morning
spilling its red ink across the skies
yet no one claims it as repulsive
it is of greater beauty;
a perfect imperfection

so don't be ashamed of your broken heart
that bleeds red,
for the breaking was just as majestic
the healing will be just as profound
and you,
even more beautiful
than the dawn

Al-Mu'id: The Restorer

the stars within your ribcage
may have lost their luster
but they will shine again
by the One who gave them light

shine on through His remembrance
and let the light spill out of your heart,
for He's placed a galaxy
inside your chest
and He can surely ignite it
once more

An-Nur: The Light

don't harden your heart
until you can't feel anymore
it is soft soil
not compacted grounds
that allows flowers to grow

Ar-Ra'uf, Al-Barr:
The Merciful & Compassionate, The Source of Goodness

i pray
that i never forget all of the times
that i raised my hands
to ask You to fill them with a rose
and was blessed to wake up instead,
to gardens upon gardens
flourishing outside

Al Mujib: The Answerer

from the details of your fingerprints
unique in their own way
to the molding of your features
and hands made of clay

just as He perfected you,
He fashioned your affairs
do not grieve,
for His single "Be!"
may answer any prayer

Al-Khaliq: The Creator

she writes about each person
that enters her life story
ink paints her heart
with words of peace and glory
her bookshelf filled,
countless covers and pages
collecting dust,
bindings engraved for ages
from "Those I've Admired"
to "Those I've Loved"
every name made immortal
every life discussed
she carefully writes
pages filled through
in hopes that the angels
will write of His love for her too

Al-Hasib, Al-Muhsi: The Accounter, The Reckoner

KNOWING YOU

oh lost soul,
do not fear

no matter how far you drift into space
He will map the constellations in your eyes
until you find Him once again

Al-Hadi: The Guide

it's me and my morals in this world full of tests
breaking and bending many others,
for we're tried to the best
yet in this world full of so many
you feel so alone
when those morals are set aside
a norm to which all are prone
but just because it's common
doesn't make it right
and just because you're alone
should not stir within you fright,
for each soul shall have what it delivers
no others will be put on the scale
it's you against yourself,
fear the Lord and you'll prevail
every stranger feels out of place
when they're away from home
this journey you travel by yourself,
yet He guides every step that you roam
when you feel out of place
or alienated during your short stay,
remember there's glad tidings to the strangers
and glad tidings coming your way

Al-Karim, An-Nafi: The Most Generous, The Bringer of Good

KNOWING YOU

her Lord preserved her heart
between the pages
of her unfinished book,

so that whoever seeks it
would have to first read
through her life
her fears
her dreams

would have to first
fall in love
with her faith
and her mind
before anything else

Al-Hafiz: The One Who Preserves and Protects

take a deep breath
and like an autumn tree
exhale your last leaf -
let go of your past mistake.

for the fall
no longer defines
you

Al-Ghaffar: The Forgiver

you're the hint of a rose
fragrance so sweet
as you rise up above
towards the Lord to meet

heavens on heavens
no pillars beneath
how strong must He be
to hold them effortlessly

at your arrival,
angels send peace on you
show you the way
to the gardens you grew

the seeds that you planted
in this life
grown into a castle
for my queen of light

you're the hint of an ocean
a sign of beauty
as you bring us back to
the shore seamlessly

waves on waves
no pillars beneath
how strong must He be
to move them effortlessly

at your arrival
angels send peace on you
show you the way
to flowing springs that run through

the gold trees planted
in that life
fruits of heaven
for my queen of light

the doors will open
to ceilings so high
reclining on couches
your princes will lie

their children will rush in
calling on you
forever awaits
in a world anew

Al-Mu'izz: The Giver of Honor

KNOWING YOU

she said she loved the rain,
so he made her drench herself in tears
she said she loved the sea,
so he had her drowning in her fears
she said she loved to fly,
so he took the ground away from beneath her feet
she said she loved to dance,
so he mesmerized her to his beat
she said she loved heights,
so he never caught her when she fell
she said she loved the stars,
so he had her hopelessly gazing through nights of hell
she said she loved laughter,
so he took it away to keep it safe with him
she said she loved the sun setting,
so he set her beaming light within
she said she loved making memories,
so he gave her unforgettable scars
she said she loved to travel,
so he coldly pushed her afar
she said she loved autumn,
so he changed colors before her eyes
she said she loved God,
so He protected her from him with His light

Al-Muhaymin: The Guardian

my dear,

don't you see the skies held up without pillars?
and the mountains made firm against the storms?
and the stars illuminating the darkness?
and the trees prostrating with the wind?

my dear,

don't you feel your heart beating without your will?
and your skin healing your deepest wounds?
and your eyes seeing the most intricate of details?
and your mind calculating the complex?

if you cannot travel the world
around you
then unravel the world
within you

Al-Mubdi, Al-Baari: The Originator, The Maker

KNOWING YOU

SHAZIYA BARKAT

Finding Me

KNOWING YOU

i have found the greatest battle
not to be that of swords and men
but that within myself

my Lord has commanded me to always be just,
but what if justice means
aiming the bullet
at my reflection
and shattering the lies and ego
that have overpowered me?

for i have become a victim of oppression
as an oppressor to myself

Al-Adl, Al-Muqsit: The Just, The Most Equitable

KNOWING YOU

i walked through the fields
of dandelions that day.
their seeds danced and floated away with the wind

they reminded me
of lost loved ones

for they, too,
were rising up home,
towards their Lord

Al-Mumit, Al-Jami: The Taker of Life, The Gatherer of Mankind

i am grateful
for the softness of a rose
and the firmness of the trees
and the strength of the winds
and the depth of the skies
and the glow of the moon

i am grateful
that even as a single drop
in the ocean of all of existence,
i reflect aspects of His greatness

Al-Badi: The Incomparable Inventor

when my worries
weigh heavy on my soul,
a merciful breeze sweeps in
and with a swift sigh,
inspires the birds within me
to spread their wings
and fly again
with full trust
in their Lord's provision

Ar-Razzaq, Al-Wahhaab: The Provider, The Giver of All

and what do i know
of the ranks of people?

she may be a lily
blossoming for her Lord
becoming more beautiful
by day
and surviving harsh storms
by night
raising herself in His eyes
even through the rain
that weighs her down

while i may be
a mimosa flower,
shrinking
closing in on myself
and turning away from my Lord
when i feel

even the slightest touch
of a raindrop

even the slightest touch
of hardship

and what do i know
of the ranks of people?

Al-Alim, Al-Khabir:
The All-Knowing, The Knower of Inner Truth

KNOWING YOU

i packed my old shoes into a box
and stored them away

what were once perfectly new
are now torn and worn out
the stitches that held them together
withering away
like my faith, with time

but i have learned
that just as we grow out of our shoes,
we grow out of who we once were
and though the past
cannot be untangled from the laces
i must not carry the dust of these shoes forever,

for each day is a chance
to start over
and tread a different path

At-Tawwaab, Al-Afuww:
The Acceptor of Return and Repentance, The Pardoner

people are stars
gleaming in my darkest times
promising guidance with their light

but the more i reach out
the more i find
how distant they truly are

and if i depend on them too much
to help me through
i may lose myself in space,
entirely.

so here i am,
trusting the Lord of the galaxies
to guide me

Al-Wakil: The Dependable

KNOWING YOU

i looked for places
to plant my garden
a place to settle
that i may call home

i dug up dirt deep within you
planting seed after seed
yet they laid there,
dry

i've found that the only garden
i need to cultivate
is within myself

the love of Him
as water to my seeds
the freedom from attachments
as the ridding of weeds,
for His nourishment
is all that i truly need

Al-Muqit, Al-Qayyum:
The Nourisher, The Self-Subsisting Sustainer of All

i am grateful
not just for that which You have given me
but for all of that which You have not

protecting me, from my own prayers

You see the completed puzzle
when i see only the pieces
i may know what i want,
but You always know what i've needed

Al-Latif, Al-Mani: The Subtly Kind, The Preventer of Harm

KNOWING YOU

i am learning
to not walk proudly on this earth,
as if my feet can move mountains
as if my strokes can outswim the rivers

for just as He exalts me with success,
He may just as easily
cause my heels
to shake the ground beneath my feet
and crumble the very foundation
that i stand upon

Al-Khaafid, Al-Mudhill: The Humbler, The Dishonorer

and perhaps the rivers run deep
and the oceans lay vast
from the inevitable tears of souls
burdened by this world

it is only
in the remembrance of my Lord
that i find relief,
for He is greater than all of my burdens,
combined

Al-Mutakabbir, Al-Kabir: The Greatest

KNOWING YOU

my faith is an anchor
to an unwavering ship
amongst the rough seas of life

i find hope
in knowing that my Lord is ever-watchful
and has certainly promised me ease with hardships
not once,
but twice

Ar-Raqib: The Watchful

and when i feel unloved
or unworthy
i place a hand on my chest
and feel my heart rising and falling
within my ribcage

it reminds me
that even when i, too, fall
it is only Him
that can raise me back up

Ar-Raafi: The Exalter

KNOWING YOU

i am guilty
of eagerly searching for blissful gardens
when it was only yesterday that i planted a seed

just as i am guilty
of impatiently seeking answers
when it was only yesterday that i made a prayer

Al-Muqaddim, Al-Mu'akhkhir: The Expediter, The Delayer

He has shown me
that just as the seas of salt and fresh water meet
but do not mix
i must always keep a balance
between my faith and this world,
for too much attachment to this earth
may cause a pure heart
to submerge in the dirt
of murky waters

Al-Quddus: The Pure One

KNOWING YOU

i must stop
my fingers
from trying to catch wealth.
it is as if attempting to grasp
intangible air

for the wind,
just like my fate,
has its own course
and sways in directions
decreed by my Lord

and who else has the power
to bring to me what i desire?

and who else has the power
to withhold from me what i long for?

Al-Ghani, Al-Mughni: The Wealthy, The Enricher

and if every word i've spoken
and every action i've committed
was written on my skin
would you still consider me
beautiful?

Ash-Shahid: The Witness

KNOWING YOU

my heart is lost
and yearns for its Creator

it is dispersed throughout the lands
in the canopies of the thick rainforests
in the solitude of the deserts
in the turbulence of the waterfalls

so if you, too, are searching
come join me.
He is closer to us
than our jugular veins
so let us find those
and trace them back
to our hearts

Ar-Rashid: The Guide

ink to my skin,
tingles creep through my veins
wanting a forever
through this temporary pain
a chaotic mess
the dots are up close
a beautiful image
from far exposed

the facade of life,
a tattoo ingrained so deep
yet a superficial image,
of which the price is too steep

an illusion from the truth
a mere amusement and play
what is it worth
if it steers me away?

Al-Haqq: The Truth

my faith
slipped through my fingers like sand
as i tried so desperately to hold on.
the comfort of its touch,
replaced by emptiness
for what seemed like forever then

i look back now
at the hourglass on my shelf
at the sand that escapes
down through the dark tunnel
plummeting to the bottom
and gathering into mountains

i look back now
at the sand above
offering me its final time
to be something more than this

i look back now
at you - my mistake,
which had managed to slip through
like a mere grain,
now hidden within the hourglass

but i will mend my ways
and no longer will i let you define me
you are minuscule.
trivial.
in relation to the mercy
of my Lord

Al-Ghafur: The Hider of Faults

when the night sky drapes above me
as a cloak
yet is unable to provide me with comfort

when the world sleeps
and the patters of my tears
are overshadowed by the rain
that pounds hard against my windows

each tear
is no less
than a conversation,
for i find Him
always listening

As-Sami: The Hearer of All

KNOWING YOU

it slammed shut
across my face
i sat there, grieving
for what felt like forever then
a traveler consumed by tears,
unaware
that though the door to this house
may have closed
the door to a kingdom
far better
had opened
across the distance

Al-Hakim, Al-Fattah: The Most Wise, The Opener

what atrocity
must have occurred

for you to curse the flesh
that taught you how to speak
for you to let go of the hands
that taught you how to hold
for you to disregard the tears
of the one who wiped yours away
for you to break the woman
who tore apart
in agony
just to enter you into this world

heaven lies
beneath the feet of mothers
so will you not then,
be grateful?

Ash-Shakur: The Grateful

KNOWING YOU

there are days
when i sit by my windowpane
and look longingly towards the pouring skies
that cleanse the earth
with drenching rain

i pull my heart from my chest and pray,
"Oh You, who is able to do all,
please cleanse the dirt from my soul
in the very same way"

Al-Qaadir, Al-Muqtadir: The All Able, The Ordainer

oh how difficult it is
to use the heat of the moment
to forge diamonds
rather than burning coal
i am still learning
to tame this rage inside of me

Al-Halim: The Calm Abiding

KNOWING YOU

there are so many times
that i have been like a child
putting my hand near the fire
in awe of its brightness and heat
not knowing
that it is when i come so close
to burning myself
that my Lord draws me away
for my own good

Ad-Dharr, Al-Muntaqim, Al-Mani:
The Corrector, The Disapprover, The Protector

an uninvited guest
settles in the valley of my heart
makes a home within my chest
and refuses to depart

the mountains of my lungs
are crumbling down beneath his weight
as he pollutes the peace once there
with oppression and hate

there are waves of emotions
that pound against my veins
lost in a whirl of wind
as they rage in a hurricane

the currents get rough
and i find myself lost at sea
within a jagged ocean as vast
as the emptiness i flee

my nights have grown longer
as i struggle to fall asleep
my days have blurred together
and my body has grown weak

tracks run over my wrist
as the departing train voices its last call
is it better to feel pain
than to feel nothing at all?

KNOWING YOU

emotions cloud my thoughts
smoke fogs up my mind
they tell me i'm not good enough
that i'm not worth it to the Divine

my faith is shaking
i can't find who I am
i am enchained by fear
as desolation takes command

saltwater shakes my core
and spills over the rims of my eyes
as the ocean drowns me
i succumb to numbness inside

i frantically glance into the distance
and find His lighthouse shining from miles away
guiding me home
from tides that make me stray

He shows me the universe;
constellations trace my skin
and even when i'm breaking,
my galaxies shine from stardust within

He shows me the dawn;
as it breaks, so do i
but there's a beauty in my breaking
as red and gold paint the morning sky

to Him i am worth more
than this world entirely
and that's all i need to overcome
my haunting thoughts of mortality

an honorable guest
has settled in the valley of my heart
He illuminates it with light
in places i've broken apart

Al-Mu'min: The Giver of Tranquility and Security

KNOWING YOU

and there are parts of me
that yearn to run away from myself
that rage against the walls of my skin
and escape the chaos that i've constructed
                                        inside

but in every direction i turn
there is You

                                  my safe haven,

from me.
and sometimes
it is in losing myself first
that
                                  i find myself
                                  through You.

Al-Wasi': The Vast, The All-Embracing

Personal Narratives & Essays

KNOWING YOU

As-Sabur: The Patient One

It's all a vivid memory. I remember those sunny afternoons filled with young, bright laughter and the arms that raised me and my cousins through our childhood days. Her gleaming eyes gazed at us as we sprinted across our backyards and recklessly swiveled bikes through the winding streets of our neighborhood. Those eyes became the lens through which we viewed our own world, a world that valued family above anything else. Yet in a moment's time, the arms that held our perfect world together became like bare winter trees, weakened from age, until they suddenly grew still.

Inna lillahi wa inna ilaihi raji'un. This common phrase, meaning *"to God we belong and to Him we shall return,"* is said often by the Muslim community after the death of a loved one. For me, that phrase didn't hit home until that day.

I never thought I'd lose my grandma that way. It was an unexpected turn of events, the first loss in our family, and a time of grief for us all. However, it was also a time of realization. It brought forth a recognition that this life is passing and as much as we would like to grip onto certain people, we must find the strength to let go and have *sabr*.

It wasn't until then that I learned about what sabr truly means. I found that sabr goes beyond just the textbook definition of patience to an enduring persistence despite any difficulties, obstacles, or discouragement that we may face. Ultimately, sabr has many layers to it.

My original idea of sabr was the patience needed when fulfilling our obligations to Allah (glory be to Him). I found this to be the *sabr* of the Prophet Muhammad (peace be upon him) as he determinedly stood in long prayers until his feet swelled up. When asked why he offered such an prayer, he responded, "should I not be a thankful slave?" From standing through nights in prayer, to fasting in Ramadan, to following the sunnah, to merely just making the five prayers a day: all of these are struggles that require perseverance as well as patience in knowing that one day we will be rewarded for our efforts.

I also found *sabr* to be the patience in refraining from sin, so as to not disobey our Creator. Living in the society we do today, there are many things that may not necessarily be encouraged in our religion. When temptations to go down a path that we shouldn't are thrown at us, how do we refrain? Fasting our eyes from what we should not see, our ears from which we should not hear, and our tongues from what we should not speak; all of these require dedication in what we believe in and hold rewards for sabr.

However, sabr extends to more than just patience in fulfilling obligations and refraining from sin. I've found that although these are important components of sabr, it is also embodied in our patience in what Allah (glory be to Him) decrees upon us, including our steadfastness in the worst of times. Life goes on despite our gains and losses, our joyous occasions and hardships, and our successes and failures. But it isn't what is thrown at us that defines us, but rather, how we *react* to those situations that defines us.

The Prophet (peace be upon him) said, *"Strange is the affair of the mu'min (the believer), verily all his affairs are good for him. If something pleasing befalls him he thanks (Allah) and it becomes better for him. And if something harmful befalls him he is patient and it becomes better for him." (Sahih Muslim 2999)*

I recognized this layer of sabr as when we remain spiritually strong through our hardships and turn to Allah (glory be to Him) in trust that He will help us get through our challenges, despite how helpless we ourselves feel. For instance, when we lose a dear friend, a family member, our wealth, or our health, we can either see it as a punishment or view it as an opportunity. To have those things that bring us joy for even a mere second in our lives are a mercy and a gift from God, even if they are later taken away. People, wealth, and possessions come and go because they were never really ours to begin with. It is through sabr that we can reap this reward of patience.

"Be sure we shall test you with something of fear and hunger, some loss in goods or lives or fruits, but give glad tidings to those who patiently persevere." (Quran 2:155)

Thus, sabr has an encompassing definition and through it, Allah (glory be to Him) provides many opportunities for us to gain rewards for patience and draw nearer to Him. Some people approach Allah (glory be to Him) through constant good deeds and acts of worship. Some have the sense and strength to avoid sin and their lack of performing many sins may be a means of drawing closer to Him.

Others may have difficulties sent onto them throughout which they are constantly patient. In this way, they may be rewarded and purified in a way equivalent to those who do good deeds or refrain from sin. And Allah (glory be to Him) knows best, for each of these are tailored through His wisdom and mercy.

So what is the ultimate sabr of the believer? That is sabr in this life, for the hereafter. It is in recognizing that this life is passing and that those bounties that we lose in this life will be replaced in the next. Therefore, we find the strength to patiently persevere every morning we wake up.

If we can practice sabr now, God-willing we will be among those to whom angels will say: *"Peace be upon you for the sabr you practiced. Excellent indeed is the final home." (Quran 13:24)*

Dhu al Jalal wa al Ikram: The Lord of Majesty and Generosity

An encouraging smile as you pass a stranger. An uplifting word to a brother or sister. A long moment of full attentiveness as a friend discloses their troubles. A period of quality time spent with the family. These may seem like mere strokes in our day, yet when observed in its entirety, these strokes come together to form the vivid painting of our lives. With each act of giving – whether it's a smile, a word, or a moment of our time – our canvas becomes rich with color.

But how you choose to decorate that canvas is up to you – it's your art. You might use a defined paintbrush, or you might smear on some color with your fingers. Creating art is not limited to just one way, as each approach ultimately forms a unique and creative piece. Use markers, stencils, crayons, or any other technique you prefer. That's the beauty of giving as well, that there are endless ways to do it. And yet each generous action ultimately adds to the exquisiteness of our canvas in the eyes of Allah (glory be to Him).

Many times when we think of giving, our minds race to the idea of monetarily giving to the less fortunate. Although as Muslims we are encouraged to give part of our earnings as *zakat* and *sadaqa*, charity is much more than that. Allah (glory be to Him)'s mercy is so vast that even if we do not have the means to give from our wealth, our generosity to others is still written as charity when we give the intangible.

The Prophet Muhammad (peace be upon him) states:
"...Enjoining good, forbidding evil, removing thorns, bones and stones from the paths of people, guiding the blind, listening to the deaf and dumb until you understand them, guiding a person to his object of need if you know where it is, hurrying with the strength of your legs to one in sorrow who is appealing for help, and supporting the weak with the strength of your arms. These are all the doors of sadaqa."

It doesn't just stop there, for even a small generous deed is never belittled in the eyes of Allah (glory be to Him). From extending your obedience and love to your parents to offering your hospitality to your guests; there are countless ways of giving. Generosity, in all its aspects, is such an immense part of our deen that our Lord specifically stresses that in order to gain His bestowments, you must first give from yourself.

"Never will you attain the good [reward] until you spend [in the way of Allah] from that which you love. And whatever you spend – indeed, Allah is Knowing of it." (Quran 3:92)

Sometimes we may consider donating and so we end up searching our houses for worn-out items or scrounge our closets for clothes we've grown out of. Although these contributions have their worth, Allah (glory be to Him) states that the utmost level of *iman* is to "spend from that which we love." Yes, it might be easier to give away those things that we don't necessarily think much of anymore, but how many times have we given away something that is truly dear to us?

Have we recently offered someone else one of our most prized possessions? What may be stopping us? This action might be difficult due to the materialistic society in which we live in today.

We are taught that if we don't accumulate materials, we'll get left behind in the race. Society says "me, me, me" while Islam says "you, you, you."

"None of you will truly believe until you love for your brother what you love for yourself." (Al-Bukhari)

When it comes down to it, generosity is one of the most noble traits of a believer as it requires selflessness from the individual. The act of giving is not only considered an act of worship, but it is much more in that it begins to mold itself as part of who we are. It allows us to grow in our empathy for others and in our love for our brothers and sisters. The act of giving forms bonds and unity. It creates the foundation for this *Ummah*. So smile and spread the love in every way you choose until your painting thrives with color.

They say beauty is in the eyes of the beholder. Will the ultimate Beholder like what He sees?

KNOWING YOU

Al-Hakam: The Judge

"I love Ramadan because that kid who never prays, prays. That girl who never covers, covers. That guy who never fasts, fasts. Even if it's just for a month, at least these 'types' of people tasted the 'sweetness of faith' just for one month. And perhaps months later down in life, if their life ever becomes bitter- they'll refer back to Ramadan and yearn for that same 'sweetness' they sampled just that one month. You call them 'Only Ramadan Muslims' but I call them 'Muslims who may only need Ramadan to change.'" - Unknown

As the blessed month of Ramadan arrives, everyone seems to be getting their Ramadan grind on: fasting, taraweeh, and dhikr. There are those who are practicing Muslims, increasing on their usual daily worship, while others struggle to pick up the Quran even once outside of Ramadan. Sometimes, as we stock up on our own good deeds, we begin to look down upon those that may find it a challenge to increase in their worship. Knowingly or unknowingly, we might begin to point out their faults: *Why does this brother not come to taraweeh prayers regularly? Why does she only wear hijab during Ramadan?*

While people are attempting to make a change in their life, their shortcomings are mocked. Rather than stressing their progress, they are criticized to such an extent that some may even give up trying. We need to keep our focus. We all have our weaknesses; no one is perfect.

Empower others to progress through love and acknowledgement of their good, not through arrogance and a condescending view of their faults.

We need to reflect on our own weaknesses to overcome them, as well as use this time to improve our own relationship with our Lord. Don't try to define where others stand, because we never really know.

There are some people I call "hidden gems." These are the ones that are not often viewed as "religious" in the public's eyes and may be the least expected to even be practicing. Yet, they are the ones to turn to God sincerely behind closed doors. This might be the sinner who has given up his bad actions and goes to God over and over again for repentance, while you judge him for a sin that has already been forgiven by his Lord. This might be that kid that doesn't show up to taraweeh prayers consistently, but he stands with *khushoo* or sincerity during long nights in prayer in solitude, while you might be yawning behind the imam. It might be the sister who doesn't wear hijab outside of Ramadan, yet she consistently makes an effort to make this Ramadan be the one that grants her enough strength to continue on with it. They are persevering. Yet, they are often misjudged. Only the One who is appreciative of even the smallest of actions, the Ultimate Judge, knows the value of their genuine efforts – hidden gems, in His eyes.

Al-Matin: The Steadfast

I stood staring at myself in the mirror, carefully wrapping my headscarf around my hair. The image stared back at me, clear as water, and that purity made me cringe. I struggle against the tide every day, against the norm of society, to fully embody the image in that mirror. I knew that it would not be as simple as draping a cloth over my head, classifying me as a Muslim. Rather, it would take the reconciliation of two very different elements of nature. I didn't truly recognize the force of the tides of islamophobia until bigotry turned into actions of hate.

On February 10, 2015, 23-year-old Deah Shaddy Barakat, his 21-year-old wife Yusor Mohammad Abu-Salha, and her 19-year-old sister Razan Mohammad Abu-Salha were murdered near the University of North Carolina Chapel Hill by 46-year-old Craig Hicks. Why? Because of their Muslim identity. Just like many of us, they were young and ambitious. They were innocent and full of dreams and passions. They had much to offer the world.

Thousands attended the funeral to remember the great spirits of the three victims. Deah, Razan and Yusor embodied what it meant to be compassionate, selfless and determined. They used what they had to give back to the community and to those across the world. *"At the end of the day,"* states Sameer Abdel-Khalek, a family friend of Barakat, *"It shows the light that persists even in darkness. You can only gauge the darkness by the light; and this light has overtaken the darkness that has befallen us."*

These three may be gone, but their light is still strong. It forces me to once again reflect on my own identity. The first time I laid the scarf on my head, there were no pins to keep it in place. The hijab, like me, was insecure. I can still remember the rapid beatings of wings in my stomach arising from doubts and societal pressures. Like most, I was raised with a standard of living, a standard of behavior and a standard of beauty. It is hard to count how many times I hesitated before finally pinning up my headscarf; I did not know how people would react. I finally became tired of trying to please others to fit in, of concealing my beliefs, and of letting false impressions of my peaceful religion spread.

After laying the cloth on my hair, I made sure the two sides were somewhat equal. I struggled with the cloth, tugging the sides, finally reaching what I aimed for. Balance. Balance between the two ends in order to fold one over the other, balance between my religion and society. I was born and raised as an American and was among the first to wear the hijab in my family; it was an unnerving experience. Still today, my peers' reactions seem to be at both sides of the spectrum. While I deal with mistrust and common misconceptions about Islam, I also find those who are accepting of my difference.

I took the ends, wrapping them around my head, making one layer at a time. The hijab embraced me. Even now, it shows me its deeper purpose as I walk through hallways, garnering curious glances from my peers: it urges individuals to look past my outer beauty and truly acknowledge my personality and morals. It covers me, reminding me of the modest woman I hope to become.

My hijab provides me with new confidence and self-respect. And today, rather than attempting to fit in with the crowd, my Muslim identity stands out as a beacon.

As I look deeper at my reflection, I see the faces of those three beautiful lives that were lost. I see Yusor. I see Razan. I see Deah. They were not too different from me. I see my identity in physical form, a constant reminder of my values.

Yes, we may continue to face challenges and crash head on into the waves. Yes, we may become overwhelmed by fears and uncertainties. Yes, we may face prejudice. But if you take more than a glance at my hijab and unravel it piece-by-piece, you will find that it is not just cloth. It serves as an identity, an unwavering symbol of universal solidarity, and a call for the end of bigotry.

KNOWING YOU

ABOUT THE AUTHOR

Shaziya Barkat, also known as s.s. barkat, is a 24-year-old writer based in New York. Her work explores themes including faith, spiritual renewal, love, loss, and mental health. Shaziya's passion for writing flourished at a young age through local poetry contests, school newspapers, and spoken word performances. During her college years, she was accepted as a staff writer for *Muslim Youth Musings,* an online literary magazine. She published "knowing You", her first collection of poetry, prose, personal narratives and essays in 2019. Aside from writing, Shaziya works as a pharmacist and freelance photographer. Stay updated with Shaziya's work on Instagram (@s.s.barkat).

KNOWING YOU

AUTHOR'S NOTE

Dear Reader,

A few years ago, I made it a personal goal to delve deeper into learning all of God's attributes and to utilize them to better myself and strengthen my faith. What began as a journey of reflecting on the names of *Allah* turned into written words during times of ease and hardship, and eventually formed this compilation. I hope that the remembrance of our Lord through this work provided you with a spiritual renewal.

Peace,
Shaziya Barkat

p.s. If you've enjoyed this work, it would mean the world to me if you can kindly leave me a book review on Amazon. It is only through readers like you that voices of writers like me are heard – your support is much appreciated. Thank you!

KNOWING YOU

ACKNOWLEDGMENTS

I would like to express my gratitude to all those that have made this book possible. Thank you to my family, friends, *Muslim Youth Musings,* and my readers for your support.

Editors:
Sadiya Barkat
Waseeya Barkat
Adam Ranginwala

Illustrations:
GreenTana

Cover Art:
ArtLana

KNOWING YOU

Made in the USA
Lexington, KY
23 November 2019